LIVING GREEN

Pollution

WORLD BOOK

a Scott Fetzer company

Chicago

www.worldbookonline.com

Editorial:

Editor in Chief: Paul A. Kobasa
Project Manager: Cassie Mayer
Writer: Robert N. Knight
Editors: Daniel Kenis, Brian Johnson
Researcher: Mike Barr
Manager, Contracts & Compliance
  (Rights & Permissions): Loranne K. Shields
Indexer: David Pofelski

Graphics and Design:

Associate Director: Sandra M. Dyrlund
Associate Manager, Design: Brenda B. Tropinski
Associate Manager, Photography: Tom Evans
Book design by: Don Di Sante
Contributing Photographs Editor: Clover Morell
Senior Cartographer: John Rejba

Pre-Press and Manufacturing:

Director: Carma Fazio
Manufacturing Manager: Steve Hueppchen
Production/Technology Manager: Anne Fritzinger

World Book, Inc.
233 N. Michigan Avenue
Chicago, IL 60601
U.S.A.

For information about other World Book publications, visit our Web site at **http://www.worldbookonline.com** or call **1-800-WORLDBK (967-5325)**.

For information about sales to schools and libraries, call **1-800-975-3250 (United States)**, or **1-800-837-5365 (Canada)**.

Picture Acknowledgments:

Front Cover: © age fotostock/SuperStock

© Alamy Images 13; © Bill Bachman, Alamy Images 33; © Corbis/Alamy Images 5; © David Hoffman Photo Library/Alamy Images 22; © David R. Frazier Photo library/Alamy Images 11; © Digital Vision/Alamy Images 30; © Michael Doolittle, Alamy Images 39; © Iain Masterton, Alamy Images 8; © Nic Miller, Organics Image Library/Alamy Images 1; © Edward Parker, Alamy Images 47; © John A. Rizzo, Photodisc/Alamy Images 48; © David Woodfall, Photoshot Holdings/Alamy Images 51; © Print Collector/Alamy Images 7; © Marcelo Rudini, Alamy Images 55; © Stuart Yates, Alamy Images 56; AP/Wide World 9, 29, 33, 34, 35, 37, 38, 42, 45, 50, 52, 57; © Jim Richardson, Corbis 10; © Getty Images 15; © AFP/Getty Images 46; © David Boily, AFP/Getty Images 28; © Liu Jin, AFP/Getty Images 44 © Daniel Piris, AFP/Getty Images 24; © Robert Sullivan, AFP/Getty Images 14; © Peter Essick, Aurora/Getty Images 6; © Radhika Chalasani, Getty Images 51; © Sean Gallup, Getty Images 18; © Ed Honowitz, Image Bank/Getty Images 54; © Pablo Bartholomew, Liasion/Getty Images 17; © John Chiasson, Liaison/Getty Images 49; © Joe Traver, Liaison/Getty Images 26, 27; © Sandro Tucci, Liaison/Getty Images 16; © Christopher Pillitz, Getty Images 13; © William Campbell, Time & Life Pictures/Getty Images 27; © Arnold H. Drapkin, Time & Life Pictures/Getty Images 31; © Cynthia Johnson, Time & Life Pictures/Getty Images 12; © Steve Liss, Time & Life Pictures/Getty Images 53; NASA 4; © John Cancalosi from Peter Arnold, Inc. 49; © Nigel Dickinson from Peter Arnold, Inc. 25; © Heldur Netocny from Peter Arnold, Inc. 15; © Tony Freeman, PhotoEdit 21; © Michael Ventura, PhotoEdit 54; © David Young-Wolff, PhotoEdit 54; © Reuters 40; © Shutterstock 32.

All maps and illustrations are the exclusive property of World Book, Inc.

Library of Congress Cataloging-in-Publication Data

Pollution.
    p. cm. — (Living green)
    Includes index.
    Summary: "An examination of pollution's causes and consequences. Includes a discussion of government and individual action that help prevent and remediate pollution. Features include fact boxes, sidebars, activities, glossary, list of recommended reading and Web sites, and index"—Provided by publisher.
    ISBN 978-0-7166-1406-7
    1. Pollution—Juvenile literature. 2. Environmental protection—Juvenile literature. 3. Sustainable living—Juvenile literature. I. World Book, Inc.
TD176.P64 2009
363.73—dc22
                            2008024116

Living Green
Set ISBN: 978-0-7166-1400-5
Printed in Mexico
1 2 3 4 5 12 11 10 09 08

The text paper of this book contains a minimum of 10% post-consumer recovered fiber.

Table of Contents

There is a glossary of terms on pages 60-61. Terms defined in the glossary are in type **that looks like this** on their first appearance in any section.

What Is Pollution?

The surface of Earth is made up of several different areas. Land describes the dry parts of Earth. Liquid water flows in Earth's lakes, rivers, and oceans. The **atmosphere** is a mixture of gases that spreads from Earth's surface to the sky far above.

While land, water, and air may seem separate, they are actually highly connected to each other. Together, they form Earth's **biosphere**, meaning all the places in which living things can dwell. Each part of the biosphere is critically important to life on Earth. If any one of the parts were to change dramatically, huge numbers of Earth's life forms would be in danger.

Natural systems keep Earth's resources healthy and clean, allowing the biosphere to support life. One example of such a system is the water cycle, which continually moves water through the three main parts of Earth's biosphere.

Today, dirt and waste produced by humans is overwhelming the natural cycles that keep the biosphere clean and healthy. Such dirt and waste is called pollution. (A single type of pollution is called a **pollutant.**) As the human population has increased and human technology—the things we make and use—has expanded, people have created more and more pollution. Because the amount of pollution is high and continues to grow, it is bringing about significant changes to the biosphere. Some of these changes threaten living things.

All pollution on Earth is interconnected, but it is helpful to think in terms of air pollution, soil pollution, and water pollution.

Air pollution is the dirtying or poisoning of the air. Materials that pollute the air are usually gases, but they can also be **particulates**—that is, tiny pieces of solid material that float freely in air.
Soil pollution is the dirtying or poisoning of Earth's thin layer of healthy, productive soil.
Water pollution is the dirtying or poisoning of any of Earth's bodies of water, from lakes, rivers, and streams to oceans.

Section Summary

Pollution is dirt or waste that enters the air, soil, or water. The amount of pollution currently produced by human activities is disrupting the natural cycles of Earth.

The burning of fossil fuels creates much of the pollution on Earth. The manufacture and disposal of goods are additional sources of pollution.

How we produce pollution

All living things produce wastes in various forms. These kinds of waste are part of the natural cycles of the biosphere. However, human societies produce vastly more pollution than communities of other living things. That is because humans, unlike other living things, are capable of building civilizations and creating technologies to solve problems. Today, human societies use huge amounts of energy to carry on modern ways of life. Most of this energy comes from burning **fossil fuels** such as coal, oil, and natural gas. Fossil fuels come from the remains of plants and animals in underground deposits that were formed millions of years ago. Burning these fuels produces much pollution, especially gases that enter the atmosphere.

Humans pollute air, soil, and water in many other ways. Our factories make objects such as cars, computers, construction materials, and clothing. The processes used in factories produce many kinds of pollution. Even growing food on farms with modern technology has led to higher pollution levels.

The following pages describe how air, soil, and water pollution are produced, and how these forms of pollution affect Earth and its living things.

Modern civilization produces vast amounts of waste. More than half of all garbage in the United States ends up in landfills.

What Is Air Pollution?

Section Summary

Air pollution affects the health of humans and the environment. The burning of fossil fuels—which include coal, oil, and natural gas—is one of the main sources of air pollution. Vehicles, factories, and power plants burn fossil fuels for energy. The burning of fossil fuels releases the gas carbon dioxide. The build-up of carbon dioxide in the atmosphere is one of the main causes of global warming.

Coal-burning power plants, like this one in Conesville, Ohio, produce large amounts of air pollution.

Air pollution occurs when any polluting gas, cloud of **particulates**, or **aerated liquid** enters the **atmosphere**. An aerated liquid is a liquid that has formed a fine spray that is light enough to stay in the air. Some of these materials may eventually fall back to the ground, but many—especially gases—become a permanent part of the atmosphere.

Earth's atmosphere forms a vital part of the **biosphere** that supports life on our planet. Living things depend upon the right mix of gases, and they especially need the gas oxygen. Over time, air pollution on a large scale brings about changes in the atmosphere, some of which may be harmful to living things.

At times in Earth's history, natural processes have changed the content of the atmosphere. For example, enormous volcanoes have spewed out trillions of tons of gases and dust. These rare events have caused changes to Earth's climate.

Today, human activities may be changing Earth's atmosphere faster than natural processes. Scientists who study the atmosphere and climate are finding that Earth's atmosphere has warmed up over the last 200 years. Most scientists believe that human activities are responsible for this change.

Some pollutants contribute to the greenhouse effect. By trapping heat from the sun, these gases cause global warming.

The build-up of carbon dioxide

The greatest change in our atmosphere has been a significant increase in **carbon dioxide** since the 1700's. Carbon dioxide is a colorless, odorless gas. Human beings and other animals give off carbon dioxide when they breathe out. Scientists estimate that the amount of carbon dioxide in Earth's atmosphere has increased by nearly 40 percent over the last 200 years. This change has been brought about mainly by burning **fossil fuels.**

Carbon dioxide helps **regulate** Earth's temperature by holding some of the sun's heat within the atmosphere. As carbon dioxide builds up in the atmosphere, it traps more and more heat. This process is called the **greenhouse effect.** Because of this effect, carbon dioxide is sometimes referred to as a **greenhouse gas.** It is not the only greenhouse gas in our atmosphere, but it is the most abundant one.

According to many scientists, the greenhouse effect is causing **global warming** on Earth today. In other words, the whole Earth is getting gradually warmer. If the Earth gets too warm, it will not be able to support many of the life forms that now live on it.

The Industrial Revolution

The Industrial Revolution was a historical process in which factories equipped with machines began to produce large amounts of goods. It began in Great Britain in the late 1780's and spread through much of Europe and the Americas over the next 100 years. The Industrial Revolution brought many benefits to society. Once goods were produced in great numbers, they became cheaper. However, factories, the energy industry, and transportation networks of the Industrial Revolution gave off huge amounts of pollution. People today are still dealing with the results of this large-scale pollution.

Engraving of a factory from 1880

AIR POLLUTION FROM AUTOMOBILES

Our modern societies depend heavily upon systems of rapid transportation. People use cars, motorcycles, buses, trains, and airplanes to travel long distances quickly. We also use ships, trains, and trucks to transport raw materials and goods. Most of these transportation methods get energy by burning some liquid form of fossil fuels. People put gasoline in their cars to drive. Huge airplanes use jet fuel. Many trucks and trains use diesel fuel. All of these energy products are made in factories from **crude oil**, the form of oil that comes out of the ground. Another name for the fossil fuel we call "oil" is **petroleum.**

Petroleum pollutants

Petroleum gives off gases and particulates when it is burned. One of these gases is carbon dioxide. Many scientists think that increasing concentrations of carbon dioxide in our atmosphere—from burning gasoline and other petroleum products—is causing global warming.

Petroleum gives off other harmful substances when it is burned. These include a poisonous, colorless, odorless gas called **carbon monoxide**, which stops the body's supply of oxygen when breathed in; **hydrocarbons** (chemical compounds containing carbon and hydrogen); and **nitrogen oxides** (compounds of nitrogen and oxygen).

Nitrogen oxides can react with sulfur oxides, which are given off when coal is burned. This forms acid, which gets incorporated into rain, creating **acid rain.** Acid rain causes damage in many ways when it falls back to the ground. Nitrogen oxides also react with hydrocarbons in the presence of sunlight to produce a form of oxygen called **ozone.**

Automobiles, like these caught in a traffic jam in Beijing, produce carbon dioxide and other air pollutants.

Smog

Ozone is the chief component of **smog,** which is one of the most widespread forms of air pollution in modern cities and suburbs. Smog is a brown, hazy mixture of gases and particulates. It develops when certain gases released by the burning of petroleum products react with sunlight in the atmosphere. This reaction creates hundreds of harmful chemicals that make up smog.

Smog is a problem in cities and suburbs of our modern world mainly because so many automobiles (cars and trucks) gather in small areas. All of these automobiles give off **exhaust** (partially burned gases) when they run.

In cities of the United States, smog became a big problem around the middle of the 1900's. Today, cities in such rapidly developing countries as China and India have serious problems with smog.

Automobiles aren't the only smog producers. In some parts of the world, motorcycles are the personal vehicle of choice. This is true in Kano, a city of about three million people in the African country of Nigeria. In Kano, two million motorcycles take part in each workday's rush hour. Many of these motorcycles use a dirtier form of gasoline than cars, so the daily motorcycle traffic in Kano ends up producing as much exhaust as six million cars. As a result, Kano has one of the worst smog problems in Africa.

Smog harms the quality of life in urban areas. It is unhealthy for anyone to breathe, but smog is especially harmful to the elderly and people who have lung disease or other health problems. City governments typically issue smog alerts when severe smog is expected. These alerts advise people to stay indoors if possible.

A cyclist wears a face mask while cycling through polluted air in Lanzhou, China. Air pollution reduced visibility to about 1,000 feet (304 meters) at the time this photo was taken.

Jet airplanes produce large amounts of exhaust, polluting the air.

AIR POLLUTION FROM PLANES, SHIPS, AND TRAINS

Along with automobiles, our modern societies also depend on aviation (air travel) and transportation by ship and by train. By and large, these forms of transportation rely on petroleum products for their energy and give off harmful exhaust.

Aviation

Jet airplanes produce huge amounts of exhaust gases. This pollution seemed manageable 50 years ago, when relatively few people flew on airplanes. Today, however, hundreds of commercial jets are in the air every day. In 1952, airlines in the United States carried 24 million passengers. In 2007, there were 677 million passengers on commercial flights in the United States.

The largest commercial jets today can carry more than 500 passengers and weigh more than 1.2 million pounds (545,000 kilograms) at liftoff. Getting that much weight in the air requires a tremendous amount of energy—energy that comes from burning petroleum-based jet fuel. Jet engines are designed to spew out hot exhaust to achieve the thrust that moves the airplane. That exhaust, like auto exhaust, contains carbon dioxide, nitrogen oxides, and particulates.

Studies have suggested that water vapor in jet exhaust could cause warming in the atmosphere over time. It seems clear that jets are an important contributor to air pollution, but their exact impact is not yet understood.

Oceangoing ships

Huge ships designed for carrying **freight** (goods) across oceans produce enormous amounts of pollution. These ships, because of their size and weight, require a large amount of energy to move. In addition, big freight ships use low-quality, cheaper fuel that burns less cleanly than such fuels as gasoline.

Large U.S. ports such as Long Beach, California, and Hampton Roads, Virginia, are most directly affected by ship pollution. Governments of many port cities are pressuring ship owners to provide auxiliary (helper) engines that burn cleaner fuel to bring the ships into port.

Trains

Most trains in the United States use diesel fuel to power their engines. Diesel fuel, like gasoline, is made from crude oil. Passenger trains are somewhat energy-efficient because large numbers of people can ride together on a single train instead of driving separate cars.

However, most train transportation in the United States is devoted to moving cargo, or freight. In 2007, there were 22,000 freight locomotives in operation on U.S. railroads, but only 270 passenger locomotives.

Locomotives spew out significant pollution in their exhaust. In one year, locomotives in the United States can give off as much nitrogen oxide as 120 coal-fired power plants and as much particulate pollution as 70 coal-fired power plants. According to some estimates, locomotives operating in the Chicago area release as much pollution as 25 million cars. Like jet planes, the number of locomotives has increased greatly since the mid-1900's, so there is much more air pollution now from this source.

Large freighters use low-quality, cheaper fuels that burn less cleanly than gasoline. This pollutes the air at such ports as Long Beach, California.

What Is Air Pollution? 11

Power plants are a major source of air pollution. Some types of power plants are cleaner than others.

AIR POLLUTION FROM POWER PLANTS

Power plants are places where electricity is generated to be sent out on wires to homes, schools, offices, stores, factories, and other consumers of electric power. Electricity itself is a "clean" energy source, but power plants can be very "dirty." That is, they can give off a lot of pollution.

How electricity is generated

To generate electricity, a force is required to push **electrons** (tiny parts of atoms) through wire circuits. In many cases, that force is provided by expanding steam. Steam in a power plant drives **turbines** (wheellike objects) to spin around and around. The turbines drive electric generators, which are machines that convert the mechanical energy into electrical energy. Because electrical energy is difficult to store, at least some power plants in the **power grid**—the interconnected system of power plants, transmission wires, and end-users of electricity—must be operating at all times.

When we use electricity, it seems like "clean" power. We simply plug in our computer or flip a light switch. There are no fumes or bad odors. However, the way in which electricity is generated determines how much pollution it creates. In the United States today, about 50 percent of electricity is generated by coal-burning power plants. Some of these plants have air pollution control equipment called **scrubbers** to filter harmful substances out of emissions, but many do not. Most of our other electric power comes from **nuclear power plants** (power plants that use nuclear energy) or **hydroelectric power plants** (power plants that use the force of moving water).

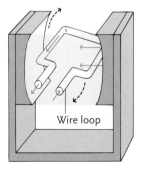
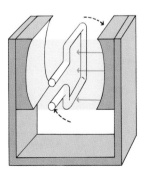
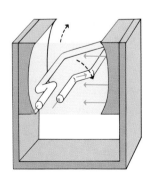

Wire loop

A simple generator consists of a U-shaped magnet and a wire loop. Rotating the wire generates an electrical current.

Coal-burning power plants

Many power plants burn coal to create the steam that drives the turbines. Coal has one tremendous advantage: It is by far the most abundant fossil fuel. In the United States, petroleum may be running out, but vast deposits of coal remain.

However, coal has a serious downside: It produces more harmful emissions than other fossil fuels, such as petroleum or natural gas. Burning coal produces carbon dioxide, nitrous oxides, and significant amounts of sulfur dioxide, an especially harmful pollutant. Sulfur dioxide, a colorless gas with a sharp odor, is harmful to living things. Breathing pollution containing sulfur dioxide irritates the lungs and windpipe and can cause serious lung disease.

Acid rain

Sulfur dioxide is the key ingredient in acid rain. When nitrous oxides and sulfur dioxide combine chemically in the presence of moisture, a solution of sulfuric acid is formed. The acid gets picked up in clouds and forms acid rain, which falls over wide areas. Acid rain damages or kills forests, poisons animals in lakes and streams, and slowly dissolves stone in buildings and statues.

Acid rain can have a devastating effect on plants, such as these trees killed by acid rain in Poland.

Oil refineries, like this one in Galveston, Texas, produce extremely toxic pollutants, some of which may cause cancer.

AIR POLLUTION FROM CHEMICAL PLANTS

In our modern world, most of the goods we use are manufactured (made in factories). In almost every manufacturing process, chemicals are used at some point. Chemicals form the basis of many products we use in our homes, too. For example, many cleaning supplies are chemicals or mixtures of chemicals.

Chemical pollutants

Many chemicals are toxic, or poisonous. Some of the chemicals used in manufacturing are gases. Chlorine is a poisonous gas. Sulfuric acid, which is used widely, readily forms sulfur dioxide, a poisonous gas. These materials can escape into the air, polluting the atmosphere. Some chemicals are **synthetic**, or human-made. Because they do not occur in nature, they can pose special pollution problems.

Most factories produce polluting emissions as **by-products** of manufacturing steps. These emissions may contain harmful gases and particulates. In the past, most chemical factories spewed all of their emissions directly into the atmosphere. Because of laws passed by governments, factories in some countries now treat their by-products to make them less toxic. However, there are still many heavily polluting factories in the world.

Refineries

A **refinery** is a factory where fuels such as gasoline and diesel are made from crude oil. Refineries use high heat and chemicals to break down the crude oil into fuel products. Like other chemical factories, they produce emissions. Some of the by-products of refining oil are particularly toxic. Among these are benzene, (*BEHN zeen*), naphthalene (*NAF thuh leen*), dioxin, and formaldehyde (*fawr MAL duh hyd*). Some of these chemicals are suspected of causing cancer.

In the United States, most refineries are in the gulf coastal areas of Texas and Louisiana. Some environmental groups claim that areas of these states near refineries have become highly polluted. The harmful effects of airborne emissions also quickly spread throughout the atmosphere.

Smelters

A **smelter** is a type of chemical factory in which metals are removed from rocky material called ore. Smelting requires applying strong chemicals or high heat to ores. Solid, liquid, or airborne by-products may be produced, many of them highly toxic. Smelters that extract sulfur from ores produce emissions containing sulfur dioxide, which can form acid rain.

Some smelters, such as the one shown below, use high heat to melt ores.

Mining and smelting take place in certain parts of the world where the metal ores are concentrated. For example, the nation of Chile in South America produces about one-third of the world's copper. Since around 1990, the Chilean government has passed laws to regulate pollution from copper smelting. These laws prohibit spewing sulfur dioxide and other harmful substances into the air.

Ozone is a form of oxygen found in harmful smog. However, ozone has a beneficial role in our atmosphere. A thick layer of ozone above Earth's surface filters out **ultraviolet rays** of sunlight, which are harmful to most living things. In the 1970's and 1980's, scientists discovered that a region of greatly reduced ozone appeared directly above the South Pole each Antarctic spring. It was found that certain chemicals produced and used by people cause the ozone hole, which continues to appear annually over the South Pole. These chemicals, called chlorofluorocarbons (CFC's), were once used widely in spray cans, air conditioners, and refrigerators. Most countries have agreed to stop making and using CFC's.

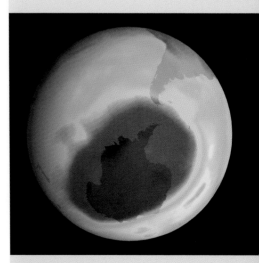

Thousands were killed and injured by an explosion at the chemical plant in Bhopal, India, in 1984.

DISASTER IN BHOPAL

Bhopal is a city of 1 million people in central India. In the 1970's, the Union Carbide Corporation, a United States company, built a **pesticide** factory in Bhopal. A pesticide is a poison that kills farm pests, such as insects.

The Union Carbide factory manufactured the chemical methyl isocyanate (*MEHTH uhl EYE soh CY uh nayt*), or MIC, to use as an ingredient in its pesticides. MIC is a poisonous gas that easily reacts with other substances. It must be handled and stored carefully.

In the early 1980's, Union Carbide suspended operations at the Bhopal factory. However, the company maintained a reduced staff to oversee the chemical plant, which still contained large amounts of toxic chemicals.

Sometime in the late evening hours of December 2, 1984, a malfunction caused water to flow into storage tanks containing MIC. This produced a chemical reaction that blew up several tanks, releasing 45 tons of MIC gas into the air.

Winds soon spread the gas over central Bhopal. People began to choke and feel nauseated, and their eyes and skin burned.

Soon, thousands were running out of their houses in panic. In the chaos, some people were trampled to death. The highly poisonous gas quickly killed thousands of people. Thousands more ran for their lives.

Word spread fast through Bhopal. Residents in parts of the city who were not seriously affected by the poison cloud also fled the city. Authorities estimated that up to 400,000 people fled in the first days after the gas leak.

No one knows for sure how many people died in Bhopal on that night. Estimates range between 3,800 and 15,000. As many as 20,000 people died weeks or months later from the effects of the gas exposure, which led to kidney and liver failure and blindness in some people. In addition, pregnant women experienced a high rate of birth defects. Many thousands of people were left seriously injured or disabled.

More than 20 years later, Bhopal still faced dangers from toxic chemicals. The Bhopal chemical plant, though locked up, still contained large quantities of toxic chemicals, according to local and international reporters. Some experts said that these chemicals were poisoning wells that provide drinking water to Bhopal's residents.

A CLOSER LOOK
Who Is Responsible?

After the Bhopal disaster, the Indian government carried out an investigation of the conditions in the Union Carbide plant. Experts discovered that safety systems in the plant had broken down. At least four automatic actions that could have prevented the explosion failed. The investigators concluded that Union Carbide officials were responsible for not maintaining the plant properly. The government of India sought compensation for the people of Bhopal. In 1989, Union Carbide agreed to pay $470 million into a fund for Bhopal residents.

The Union Carbide plant in Bhopal

Some power plants, such as this one in Germany, burn garbage to generate electricity.

AIR POLLUTION FROM WASTE DISPOSAL

Years ago, people all across the United States raked fallen leaves in the autumn season and burned them. As with burning fuels, the burning of leaves spews pollution into the air. This pollution consists of carbon dioxide, particulates (soot), and other materials. Today, most communities collect raked leaves from homeowners and compost them (pile them up to turn them into soil additives over time).

Hazardous waste incineration

Incineration means burning thoroughly. Although most communities have stopped or cut down on burning leaves and trash, some **hazardous wastes** must be incinerated. Hazardous wastes are materials that can endanger human health or damage the environment. Such wastes are incinerated in specially designed hazardous waste incinerators, which provide extremely high heat and have special features to sift harmful materials out of their emissions. In the United States, hazardous waste incinerators are regulated by the **Environmental Protection Agency (EPA)**, the federal agency that works to protect the U.S. environment from pollution.

A hazardous waste system consists of a kiln (oven that produces very high heat), an afterburner (a second furnace that burns material left from the kiln), and an air pollution control system, also called the scrubber. It filters out harmful pollutants from emissions.

One common kind of hazardous waste is medical waste from hospitals and clinics. It consists of blood, body tissues, or by-products of bodies. Because medical waste contains bacteria and viruses, it could spread disease. Incineration kills all harmful germs in medical waste.

Some environmental groups claim that hazardous waste incinerators are not safe enough to use. They point out that despite the use of scrubbers, some harmful pollutants still get into the air. They also express concern about small amounts of the pollutants that collect in the kiln itself.

Landfills

In the United States, more than half of all the garbage collected ends up in **landfills**. A landfill is a place where trash and other solid wastes are deposited. After the waste is dumped, special machines compact it (press it tightly together). The landfill gradually builds up in height as more and more layers are added.

Inside a landfill, bacteria and chemical reactions produce gases over time, especially carbon dioxide and methane. Both carbon dioxide and methane are greenhouse gases that trap heat in Earth's atmosphere. Landfill gases may also contain traces of toxic materials such as mercury. Small amounts of mercury are used in batteries, fluorescent light bulbs, paints, and other materials that end up in landfill waste.

Unless a landfill is carefully sealed, the gases will escape into the air. In a sealed landfill, gases typically push into the soil underneath and work their way elsewhere through porous rock. In some cases, methane escapes underground and collects in hollow spaces or buildings. Because methane catches fire easily, concentrated methane can cause an explosion. Apart from this danger, landfill gases are often foul (bad-smelling).

Toxic gases can escape landfills through the air and through the soil.

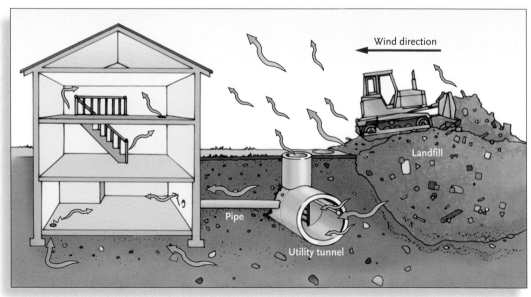

Source: U.S. Department of Health and Human Services, Agency for Toxic Substances and Disease Registry.

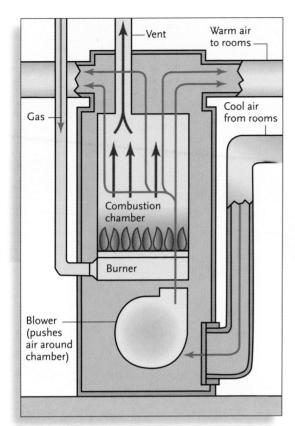

A typical home furnace produces carbon dioxide and other air pollutants.

AIR POLLUTION FROM HEATING

In many parts of the world, people use indoor heating during cooler seasons. In times past, the burning of wood or coal provided indoor heat. Today, much of our indoor heat comes from furnaces that burn natural gas or heating oil from petroleum. In houses with such furnaces, a pipe or tube called a vent carries exhaust from the furnace to the outside air. This exhaust contains many of the same pollutants that come from cars, trucks, and airplanes. The main element of the exhaust is carbon dioxide.

The furnace exhaust from an average house is a fairly small amount. But taken together, the huge number of heated buildings in the world are significant contributors to greenhouse gases in our atmosphere.

Heated buildings vary widely in size, from small houses to large public buildings and discount stores. Gigantic skyscrapers require fuel for heating on an even larger scale. The table below compares sizes of the floor space of several heated structures.

Many public and commercial buildings are large polluters. Today, the owners and managers of many such buildings search for ways to reduce energy use and emissions.

Structure	Area, square feet	Area, square meters
Average studio apartment *	500	47
Average new U.S. home	2,350	218
Merchandise Mart, Chicago	4,200,000	390,000
Sears Tower, Chicago	4,400,000	409,000
The Pentagon, Arlington, Virginia	6,500,000	604,000

* one larger room plus a bathroom

Indoor air pollution

The air that we breathe indoors comes from the outside air, so it carries any pollutants that exist in outside air. The air also picks up more pollutants inside buildings. When air becomes trapped inside for a period of time, the pollutants can become more and more concentrated.

To provide healthy environments, buildings need to have good **ventilation**—that is, a regular exchange of stale air for fresh air. However, many buildings today are designed to be shut up most of the time, with heating in winter and air conditioning in summer. This situation has led to a problem called **sick building syndrome**, or **SBS**. Sick building syndrome occurs when air inside a building is continually stale and polluted. People working in SBS environments experience symptoms such as headache, burning eyes, throat irritation, dry cough, dizziness, nausea, and fatigue (tiredness).

Reversing SBS in a building often requires the assistance of air quality specialists. These experts examine the building to find out where the pollutants are coming from and why the ventilation is not working. "Curing" a building of SBS can be costly and time-consuming.

Another potential danger in buildings is carbon monoxide poisoning. Carbon monoxide is especially dangerous because it has no color or odor, so it is difficult for people to detect. Furnaces in houses and other buildings give off carbon monoxide. If the vent that carries away exhaust is blocked up, the carbon monoxide can get trapped in living areas.

Carbon monoxide poisoning kills people. In rare cases, whole families have died at night in their home when carbon monoxide built up inside. Because of this danger, safety experts advise people to keep carbon monoxide detectors in their homes. If something goes wrong with the furnace and carbon monoxide builds up, the detector makes a loud noise.

Safety experts advise people to use carbon monoxide detectors in the home.

What Is Soil Pollution?

Section Summary

Soil pollution harms Earth's thin layer of healthy, productive soil. Factories, mines, and farms are a few of the major polluters of soil. Examples of soil pollution include chemical or oil spills at factories, accidents at nuclear power plants, the removal of soil at an open mine, and the use of human-made chemicals to grow crops. Soil pollution can lead to water pollution when it seeps into the ground and enters nearby water sources.

Soil pollution can be devastating to living things. The soil shown here has been contaminated with the heavy metal lead.

Soil pollution involves the poisoning of Earth's thin layer of healthy, productive soil. Healthy soil is an extremely important resource, for it is where much of our food is grown. Without fertile soil, farmers could not grow enough crops to feed the world's people.

Healthy soil includes countless living organisms such as bacteria, fungi, and small animals such as insects and worms. These living things help break down wastes in the soil and release nutrients. Soil also contains air, water, and such minerals as sand and clay. There are many kinds of soil, each with unique characteristics that determine how well crops can grow.

Soil forms slowly, but it can be destroyed quickly. Many kinds of pollution can kill the organisms living in soil, harming the soil's ability to support crops. In addition, such modern processes as mining can strip healthy soil from land.

Soil pollution and water

Rainwater washes soil pollution into bodies of water such as creeks, rivers, and lakes. In this way, soil pollution may spread into waterways and become water pollution. In time, this pollution reaches Earth's oceans.

Pollutants in soil can also contaminate drinking water supplies that come from **ground water.** In some areas of Earth, there is enough water beneath the surface to supply drinking water for nearby cities and towns. People dig wells to reach these areas of water. Ground water supplies 20 percent of the fresh water used in the United States, so it is especially important to keep it clean.

Ground water is held in a layer of porous rock that sits on top of a layer of watertight rock or other material. When it rains or snows, water seeps into the soil and accumulates in ground water, raising the water table (level of water). Pollution that soaks into the soil may eventually end up in ground water. Wells that tap into the ground water then become polluted.

Soil pollution that reaches ground water can wash downstream into rivers, lakes, and oceans.

Land surface

Surface water

Water table

Ground water

Source: U.S. Geological Survey.

SOIL POLLUTION FROM FACTORIES

Factories make many products that we use. Our modern lifestyle would not be possible without **industrial production,** the process of making goods on a large scale. However, most factories produce some kinds of pollution along with their products. Most of this pollution can be reduced or cleaned up, but not all factory owners have taken responsibility to do so.

Factories can produce toxic chemicals that are very dangerous to people. These inspectors in Paraguay must wear special protective suits to inspect toxic waste.

Factories can pollute air, soil, or water, depending upon what they make and where they are located. Pollution from one factory can spread to many other areas on Earth.

Toxic chemicals

Factories use many chemicals to make the products we use. For example, computers are made of plastic, metal, glass, and other materials. Numerous chemicals and steps are required to make each of these materials. Some of the chemicals mixed into these materials are toxic by themselves. Companies buy these chemicals and often store them in large metal drums (barrels) in the factory or near it. Although the drums are made to be sturdy, accidents sometimes happen and toxic chemicals leak out. Also, if the factory owners are not careful, the drums may corrode (rust out) over time. Keeping storage drums and other equipment in good shape is one example of the responsibilities that factory owners have to keep pollution as low as possible.

After chemicals are used in a factory process, factories must dispose of them. Factories, especially in the past, have dumped these chemicals into streams or holding ponds near the factory. The toxic chemicals seep into the surrounding soil and, eventually, into ground water. In addition, the chemicals at ground level can aerate, or turn into tiny particles that breezes pick up and carry into the **atmosphere.** In these ways, soil pollution can spread throughout Earth.

GREEN FACT

Up until the 1900's, hat makers used a mercury solution to make the animal hairs in the material for hats more flexible. The expression "mad as a hat-ter" comes from the many hat makers who became mentally ill from exposure to mercury.

Chemicals used at factories, such as this cement factory in France, can pollute nearby soil and water.

Heavy metals

Heavy metals such as lead, mercury, and arsenic are especially toxic to humans and other living things. Such metals were once common in manufactured products and factory processes. For example, lead was once widely used in paint and gasoline. Lead poisoning can occur in children who eat paint chips that have flaked from older painted surfaces.

Some factory processes still involve these metals, though researchers are finding ways to reduce their use. Lead and mercury easily spread from soil to water and air and cause pollution that lasts a long time. These heavy metals do not break down naturally and can collect in the tissues of animals. In human beings, heavy metals can damage bones, various internal organs, and the nervous system. They may also cause cancer.

Tanks leaked toxic waste into the soil under Love Canal, New York, making the town uninhabitable.

A POLLUTED COMMUNITY

Pollution affects most of the world's people in one way or another. However, some places bear a greater burden of pollution than others. About 30 years ago, the name "Love Canal" became a household word in the United States for the dangers of extreme local pollution.

In Niagara Falls, New York, a housing subdivision was developed on land previously owned by the Hooker Chemicals and Plastics Corporation. The new neighborhood was called Love Canal after a partially built canal on the land. During the 1940's, Hooker operated a chemical plant there, dumped about 22,000 tons of chemical waste into the Love Canal, and turned the canal into a **landfill.**

The residents of Love Canal believed that their neighborhood was as safe as any other in the country. Then in the mid-1970's, unusually heavy rains and snows hit the area. Rainwater and melting snow flushed out chemicals buried in the shallow landfill. Residents began to smell strong chemical odors and see chemicals oozing into their basements. They realized that something was wrong.

New York state officials sent pollution experts into the Love Canal area. These scientists discovered traces of 421 chemicals in the soil there. One local boy died at age seven of kidney disease, which doctors believed was caused by exposure to toxic chemicals. A variety of illnesses affected other Love Canal residents, including a high number of problems with pregnancies and birth defects.

In 1978, the state of New York offered to buy up the homes at the center of the Love Canal development so that residents could move out and buy homes elsewhere. In 1980, the federal government under President Jimmy Carter extended the buyout to include all Love Canal residents. After the people left, state and federal agencies began cleaning up the toxic site.

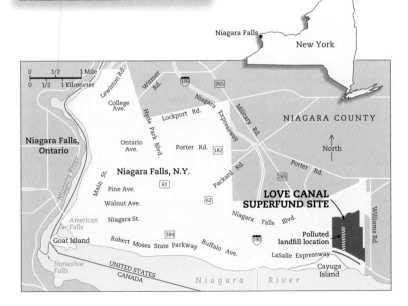

Residents of Love Canal, New York, were unaware of the dangers posed by toxic chemicals buried underneath the ground.

A CLOSER LOOK
The Hero of Love Canal

In 1978, Love Canal resident Lois Gibbs became worried when her children were getting sick constantly. When she read a story about Love Canal's history as a chemical waste dump, she organized her neighbors to find out the truth about Love Canal and to seek help from the New York state government. Gibbs and others pressed state officials to conduct a study of the pollution. When the study made clear that Love Canal was a toxic environment, Gibbs campaigned for government support to relocate Love Canal residents. After a long fight, she and her neighbors succeeded. The Love Canal story became a national sensation. As a result, the U.S. Congress in 1980 passed the "Superfund" law, a plan to detoxify polluted sites around the United States.

What Is Soil Pollution? 27

Mines, such as this uranium mine in Canada, can pollute both soil and water.

SOIL POLLUTION FROM MINING

Our modern societies use many materials that come from underground. Coal, oil, and natural gas, which are mined or drilled from the ground, provide most of our energy. We use metals such as copper, iron, tin, nickel, gold, and silver in many products. We also cut stone from quarries to use as building materials. Activities that extract (dig out) these materials from the ground are known as mining.

Mining disturbs the ground and the soil. A form of coal mining called strip mining strips off layers of topsoil to expose the coal. When all the coal is taken out of the mine, a barren, infertile wasteland is left. That is why many laws were passed in the United States during the 1900's that required owners of mining companies to refill used-up strip mines with fertile soil and plant trees and other plants. The plants' roots hold the soil fast and help to prevent **erosion.**

Humans have mined parts of Earth for thousands of years, but only within the last 50 years or so have scientists fully understood the pollution mines cause. Mining activities have heavily polluted some places in the world.

In southeastern Germany, mines have been operating in the Vils River Valley since 1427. These mines produced lead and other heavy metals. As a result, soils that have drifted downstream from the mines contain concentrations of these heavy metals. Scientists are studying these deposits to determine how harmful they might be to the people who live nearby.

Similarly, in the Coeur d'Alene (*KUR duh LAYN*) River Valley in Idaho, the mining of lead and other heavy metals began in 1889 and has since polluted much of the floodplain. Researchers had found high levels of lead in the bloodstreams of children living in the area, raising concerns that these children might suffer from brain or kidney damage.

During the era of the Soviet Union, a city in Siberia called Norilsk produced huge amounts of nickel. World demand for nickel is high because it is a key ingredient of stainless steel. The nickel mines and **smelters** in the Norilsk region poured out wastes that polluted air, soil, and water. During its period of high production, the Norilsk nickel complex spewed out more sulfur dioxide than all of France. The smelters also dumped tons of sludge on the ground around Norilsk. Today, there is so much nickel left in the sludge that people are reprocessing it to extract and sell the valuable metal.

A nickel smelter in Norilsk, Russia, produced tons of sludge that polluted the surrounding soil.

A CLOSER LOOK
Smelting

Soil pollution caused by smelting can contaminate nearby water sources. When metal is separated from ores and rocks in the smelting process, it creates wastewater and solid **by-products,** called slag. Some of these wastes are very strong acids. Other are extremely toxic poisons called cyanides.

Factories must dispose of these substances, which can poison the soil around a mine and leak into streams or ground water. This can have disastrous results for most living things.

SOIL POLLUTION FROM ENERGY USE

Today's economy uses huge amounts of energy. We use energy to move from place to place, to make things in factories, and to heat and power homes and offices. We also use energy to run information systems such as computers, phones, and satellite networks.

Energy comes from many different sources. At present, most of our energy comes from burning **fossil fuels** such as oil. Some of our energy comes from **nuclear power plants** and some from windmills, underground steam, sunlight, and other sources.

When gasoline and other toxic chemicals leak from underground tanks, they contaminate soil and water.

Transporting and storing oil

The world's shorelines are at risk of pollution by oil tankers, huge ships that transport oil to consumers. If such a tanker becomes damaged at sea or sinks, vast amounts of oil can spill into seawater and wash up on nearby shores. The oil pollution taints coastal soil and sickens and kills many species of animals. Since the mid-1900's, a number of such accidents have occurred.

Oil and oil products, such as gasoline, are often stored in drums or tanks at or below ground level. Like **crude oil**, gasoline contains a number of toxins, so preventing it from spilling and seeping into soil is extremely important. In 2003, an underground tank at a filling station near St. Paul, Minnesota, sprang a leak and released 3,000 gallons (11,356 liters) of gasoline into the ground. The gasoline ran into a storm sewer, which channeled it to a wetland area. Removing the gas and cleaning up the wetland cost thousands of dollars and required help from state and federal environmental agencies.

Nuclear power

A nuclear power plant draws energy from radioactive material in fuel rods that make up part of the nuclear reactor, or engine. The energy produced by the fuel rods turns water into steam, which drives the **turbines** of the generating plant.

If the fuel rods are allowed to get too hot, they could melt a hole in the sturdy container around the reactor and plunge into the ground underneath the plant. That, in turn, would cause an explosion of ground water that would spray dangerous radioactive material into the surrounding areas.

An accident similar to this happened in Chernobyl, Ukraine, in 1986. At that time, Chernobyl was part of what was then the Soviet Union. The nuclear plant released radioactive materials that were picked up by winds and carried across much of eastern and northern Europe. Radioactive dust settled out of the clouds on the ground below. Hardest hit was Belarus, an eastern European country then part of the Soviet Union. The nuclear contamination made 494,000 acres (200,000 hectares) of farmland completely unusable in that country. Most of it was still unusable 20 years later. The radioactive cloud also contaminated forests in Belarus.

Disposing used-up nuclear fuel is another environmental challenge. Such fuel is not useful, but it remains radioactive and must therefore be stored in extremely thick, sturdy containers. Over time, the containers of used-up fuel pile up in special storage buildings near nuclear power plants.

In 2002, the U.S. Congress approved a plan to store thousands of tons of nuclear waste in a special chamber underneath Yucca Mountain in Nevada. Many U.S. citizens oppose the plan.

Chernobyl power plant

The Chernobyl accident polluted large parts of Ukraine, Belarus, and Russia. This map shows ground contamination by cesium-137, a radioactive form of the element cesium, given in units of radioactivity called curies.

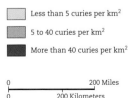

☐ Less than 5 curies per km²

☐ 5 to 40 curies per km²

■ More than 40 curies per km²

0 ——— 200 Miles
0 ——— 200 Kilometers

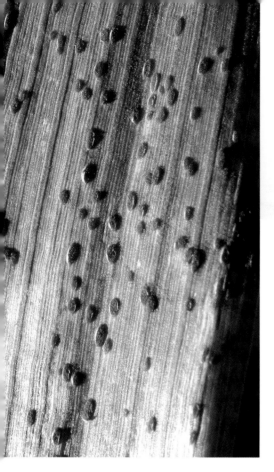

Farmers use chemicals to kill fungi, such as rust. Those chemicals often make their way into people's drinking water.

SOIL POLLUTION FROM AGRICULTURE

Agriculture includes all the ways in which people raise crops and animals for food and other products, such as **biofuels.** Biofuels are liquid fuels made from plant materials. One of the most widely used biofuels is **ethanol**, an alcohol made from corn or sugar cane.

Farming with chemicals

Today's farmers produce far more food and other products than ever before in history, but at a great cost to the environment. Some farmers try to avoid using chemical additives to grow their crops, instead relying on natural **fertilizers** and pest control methods. However, many modern farmers put large amounts of chemical fertilizers in their soil to speed the growth of crops. They also use chemical **pesticides** (poisons that kill insects), **fungicides** (poisons that kill fungal pests), and **herbicides** (poisons that kill weeds).

Most of these substances are chemicals made in factories. Over time, these strong chemicals wash from fields into streams and are carried into rivers, bays, and the ocean. Both on farmland and in waterways, agricultural chemicals bring about many unintended results.

Some agricultural poisons end up in the water that people drink. The World Health Organization (WHO), an agency of the **United Nations (UN)**, has estimated that there are 1 million cases of pesticide poisoning every year throughout the world. Various kinds of agricultural poisons can cause nerve damage, cancers, birth defects, liver damage, thyroid disease, and perhaps even diabetes.

Often, many agricultural chemicals go unused and end up stored in unsafe places. This problem has led to dangerous pollution in some countries of Africa. In Mali alone, an estimated 22,440 gallons (85,000 liters) of pesticides are stockpiled. Leakage from these stockpiles has polluted a number of wells for drinking water in the country. In the 1990's, pesticides intended for use on cotton crops in the African country of Ghana were used instead on food crops. People who ate the food were at risk of pesticide poisoning.

Deforestation

A different kind of agricultural pollution happens when people cut down too many trees to clear land to grow crops for food or fuel. Tree roots help hold soil in place. Tree or other plant cover are also necessary to keep the land healthy.

In Haiti, an island in the West Indies, people have cut down almost all the trees to use as fuel. The loss of trees in this hilly land has caused the loss of soil through erosion. Now there are few areas of Haiti fertile enough to grow good crops.

The loss of trees has also contributed to worsening floods and mudslides in Haiti. In May 2004, several days of heavy rains caused massive flooding on the island and resulted in the deaths of 1,059 people.

Workers dig a canal as part of an effort to reforest Haiti. The removal of trees can erode soil and lead to floods and landslides.

A CLOSER LOOK
Salt Can Pollute, Too

Too much salt can poison soils just as much as toxic chemicals. An excess of salt can end up in soil when irrigation is constantly used on farmland. With irrigation, farmers transport water to their land from an outside source, such as a lake or stream. If the water used is slightly salty, over time the salt will build up in the soil. The salt concentration may reach a level toxic enough that nothing will grow. Salt build-up is a problem in some farmland in the southwest United States. In Nevada, California, Arizona, and Utah, far more than half of all farmland is irrigated. Farmers there must monitor salt levels in irrigation water to protect their soil from damage.

What Is Water Pollution?

Section Summary

Water pollution harms all of Earth's bodies of water. Water can be dirtied with human and animal wastes, chemicals, and oil. Pollutants that enter water sources can poison every level of the food chain. Water pollution that starts in one source, such as a stream or river, can eventually reach larger bodies of water, such as oceans. Plastic trash in the oceans is another example of water pollution.

Crude oil washes ashore in Beirut, Lebanon. Water pollution can travel far from its source.

About 71 percent of Earth's surface is covered by ocean water. Water also rests or flows on land in the form of lakes, ponds, rivers, and streams. About 97 percent of all the water on Earth is salty. Only 3 percent is fresh (free of salt), and much of that fresh water is locked up in ice at Earth's north and south poles.

All forms of life on Earth require water to live. The oceans are rich with life, and on land, life tends to cluster around watery or moist places. Having access to unpolluted water is critical to every human being and all other living things on Earth.

Water pollution occurs when human activities cause water to become dirtied with human and animal wastes, toxic chemicals, metals, oils, or other harmful materials. Waters anywhere on Earth—in lakes, rivers, the oceans, or **ground water**—can become polluted.

Pollution spreads from one part of Earth to another. For example, harmful chemicals that have contaminated soil are washed into streams by rain. Then the pollution becomes water pollution. Also, air pollution easily becomes water pollution when rain collects **pollutants** as it forms in clouds and then falls into bodies of water.

The oceans

All of Earth's water is connected, but ocean water makes up a unique **habitat**, or place where living things dwell. Oceans exist in cold polar areas of the world as well as warm tropical areas. Oceans differ from other watery places in many ways. For example, ocean water is salty. The oceans are also far deeper than any other bodies of water on Earth.

Earth's huge and varied oceans are home to countless numbers and kinds of living things. Like other water, ocean waters can become polluted. Earth's oceans are changing today because of human-caused pollution. These changes threaten the survival of some species.

Fresh water

Most land-dwelling plants and animals require fresh water to live. Because only about 3 percent of Earth's water is fresh—and much of that is locked up in polar ice—fresh water is a precious resource on Earth. Obtaining potable (usable) drinking water is a pressing challenge for many of the 6.6 billion people on Earth. When human societies pollute carelessly, the amount of fresh drinking water available shrinks even further.

Polluted water in rivers and lakes can kill fish and other wildlife.

Water pollution can travel far downstream, contaminating other bodies of water.

WATER POLLUTION FROM CHEMICALS

Today's world is awash in human-made chemicals. We use chemicals in factories, as cleaning products, in medicines and cosmetics, in agriculture, and for many other purposes. With all these chemicals around, it is not surprising that some of them end up in our rivers, streams, lakes, and oceans, as well as in ground water.

For 150 years after the start of the Industrial Revolution in the 1780's, people had little understanding of the impact of pollution on bodies of water. Since the mid-1900's, however, people have become increasingly aware that Earth's water is a precious and fragile resource.

The threat to human health

Water pollution is a complex problem. All bodies of water on Earth are connected in one way or another. Rivers and streams flow into bays, gulfs, and oceans. Even isolated lakes are connected with other bodies of water through ground water. Water pollution can spread far and wide.

One of the most basic needs of humans and animals of all kinds is clean drinking water. However, because pollution spreads so easily through water, many of the world's people must drink water that is polluted with waste, germs, or chemicals. According to the World Health Organization (WHO), almost half the population in sub-Saharan Africa (the part of the continent south of the Sahara desert) was without reliably clean drinking water in the early 2000's.

Polluted fish and seafood

Toxins in water tend to spread through the **food chain** of marine animals. The food chain is a group of interrelated organisms that eat each other. In the ocean, most food chains begin with tiny organisms at the surface that make food from the sun's energy. These organisms are eaten by other organisms, which are then eaten by small fish. Big fish eat the little fish, right up to the largest predators in the ocean.

Toxic chemicals tend to become concentrated in the bodies of fish high in the food chain. Small amounts of chemicals may cause little harm to the tiny organisms at the bottom of the ocean's food

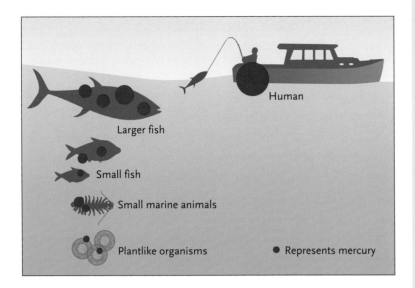

Larger fish

Human

Small fish

Small marine animals

Plantlike organisms

● Represents mercury

On June 22, 1969, the residents of Cleveland, Ohio, were amazed to see the Cuyahoga River alight with flames. The city's many manufacturers had for decades been dumping chemicals in the river. According to local reporters, the fire started when sparks from a railroad train ignited an oily patch in the river. Though this was not the first time the Cuyahoga River caught fire, it was widely reported and brought national attention to the problem of water pollution. This event was an important factor in the passage of the U.S. Clean Water Act of 1972, which regulated the wastes that industries could release into streams and rivers.

chain. But even small amounts of chemicals can accumulate as fish eat the smaller organisms and are eaten by even larger fish.

Mercury can become concentrated in animals that are high on the food chain.

In the late 1950's and 1960's, the problem of fish tainted by pollution was demonstrated dramatically in Japan. People in the coastal community of Minamata depended on locally caught fish for their diet. In the late 1950's, a strange and frightening disease began to spread through Minamata. It caused people to suffer severe brain damage and paralysis (inability to move). After a long investigation, researchers discovered that fish eaten by Minamata residents were highly polluted with mercury. They found that a local chemical factory had been dumping mercury-tainted waste into Minamata Bay since 1932.

Engineers and pollution experts began work to clean up Minamata Bay in 1968. However, little could be done for the people who had already suffered mercury poisoning.

Mercury pollution is still a cause for concern. In 2004, the U.S. Food and Drug Administration (FDA) issued an advisory (statement of caution) urging pregnant and nursing women to limit their eating of such ocean fish as mackerel and swordfish.

Water pollution from smelters

A **smelter** is a chemical plant in which metals are extracted from rocky ore. Smelters are connected with mining operations. The smelting process typically involves high heat or strong, toxic chemicals such as cyanide or sulfuric acid.

Most ores contain only tiny bits of the desired metal. As much as 99 percent of an ore, by weight, can be waste. This waste, suspended in a toxic soup of chemicals—usually including poisonous **heavy metals**—is sometimes stored in above-ground ponds called **tailings ponds**. Tailings are ground-up solid wastes from smelting. Often, the wastewater in tailings ponds becomes more and more acidic (acid-containing) over time. This is because ore contains compounds of sulfur, which react with air and water to produce sulfuric acid. This highly poisonous wastewater soaks into surrounding soil. It can also pour into streams and rivers through carelessness or accidents.

A river in Oklahoma runs orange after a flooded mine released acidic wastewater and heavy metals.

Residents of Picher, Oklahoma, near the center of a region of lead and zinc mines, have been accustomed to seeing and smelling sour, bright orange water running in a creek through their town. The mines in the area closed in 1970, but the pollution they created remains. By the early 2000's, most of the residents of Picher had been moved to other communities, with help from the federal government. Meanwhile, the **Environmental Protection Agency (EPA)** and other government agencies were attempting to clean up the pollution.

Water pollution from POP's

POP's, or **persistent organic pollutants**, are a group of 16 dangerous human-made **organic chemicals** (chemicals that contain carbon atoms). POP's do not break down easily, spread quickly through water, and build up in body tissues. Many POP's are insect-killing **pesticides** that have been found to be dangerous to many other life forms. One POP, dioxin, is a **by-product** of incinerating certain industrial chemicals.

Polychlorinated biphenyl, or PCB, is an especially harmful POP. Scientific studies have shown that PCB's may cause birth defects, cancer, liver damage, and nerve disorders. PCB's have spread so widely that they have even been found in the fat of Antarctic penguins. In 1979, the United States government prohibited production of PCB's. Since then, many other nations have also acted.

Water pollution from medical drugs

Today, there are thousands of medical drugs available to treat or prevent disease. These chemicals sometimes get into ground water and streams through human waste flushed into sewers. One such chemical is estrogen, which is found in women's birth control pills. Estrogen is a type of biological chemical called a hormone. It affects the **reproductive** systems of organisms.

In 2007, Canadian scientists reported that some fish living in the wild were being exposed to this estrogen and, as a result, were developing abnormally. Some male fish began producing hormones that should be produced only by females. In females, the estrogen slowed down or stopped egg production. The scientists warned that increasing levels of estrogen in waterways could lead to reductions in fish populations.

Scientists are increasingly concerned that water pollution is causing deformities and even extinctions among water-dwelling animals. Water pollution may have caused the deformity (incorrect shape) of this frog's back leg.

DEATH IN THE RIVERS

Rivers are a critical part of Earth's life-supporting **biosphere.** They drain land masses of rainwater and thus form an important link in the water cycle. In their natural state, rivers are full of many forms of life, including plants, fish, snails, and other small animals. Rivers provide transportation and drinking water to human communities.

A **river system** is a river and all the tributaries (smaller streams) that flow into the river. Rivers systems typically drain large areas of land. One such river system is the Danube system in Eastern Europe. One of the Danube's main tributaries is the Tisza River. The Tisza and

Dead fish collect along the Tisza River in the country then known as Yugoslavia after cyanide and other pollutants spilled from a gold mine in Romania.

the lower Danube drain parts of Hungary, Romania, Croatia, Serbia, and Bulgaria.

In late January 2000, a dam holding a tailings pond at a mine near Baia Mare, Romania, broke, spilling 26 million gallons (100 million liters) of liquid poisons into a small tributary of the Tisza River. This tainted water flowed into the Tisza, which carried the poisons downriver to its junction (meeting) with the Danube River. From there, the poisons flowed all the way down the Danube to the Black Sea. This journey of nearly 800 miles (about 1,250 kilometers) took about one month.

The most concentrated poison in the tailings pond was cyanide, one of the deadliest poisons known. The cyanide wave swept down the rivers, killing everything in its path. At some places in the Tisza River, experts measured concentrations of cyanide 700 times the level considered safe for living things. The three countries most directly affected were Romania, Hungary, and Serbia (then Yugoslavia).

Many millions of fish died in the disaster. Most of the dead fish were removed and burned or buried. The environmental minister of Hungary estimated that there were 1,240 tons of dead fish in the Tisza River in Hungary in the wake of the cyanide

flow. Experts estimated that it would take years for some of the fish populations to recover, if at all. Romania, Hungary, Serbia, and Bulgaria had well-established fishing industries on the rivers, and these were shut down indefinitely.

Drinking water was also threatened by the cyanide poisoning. As the cyanide wave approached Szolnok, Hungary, authorities there shut down the city's water plant, which drew water from the Tisza River. Similar actions in other communities limited human exposure to the poison. In the region around Baia Mare, Romania, however, experts warned that drainage from the tailings pond was probably leaching into wells that provided drinking water. Although no human deaths were reported in the disaster, long-range effects of the poison on people in the affected areas were unknown.

Cyanide breaks down quickly in nature, and in the end, parts of the river system recovered from the cyanide pollution. However, heavy metals such as lead and arsenic were measured in high concentrations in the rivers' mud beds at a number of locations. Environmental experts were unsure what impact this pollution would have over the long term.

The lesson of Baia Mare was clear, however. A single industrial plant with lax or failing safety controls can spread death and ruin throughout an entire river system of hundreds or thousands of miles.

Pollution from a tiny tributary of the Tisza River eventually made its way into the Danube River and the Black Sea.

Local residents collect buckets of crude oil after a spill in South Korea. Cleaning up such oil spills is difficult and expensive.

WATER POLLUTION FROM ENERGY INDUSTRIES

Many of the ways we generate and use energy produce pollution of Earth's air and soil. Our energy use also poses a threat to Earth's waters.

One of our most important energy resources is **petroleum**, or oil, a **fossil fuel.** Oil is drilled from the ground in places scattered around the globe. Oil-rich areas include the Arabian peninsula, the North Sea, Russia, Venezuela, and Nigeria. These places are often far from the heavily populated regions that use most of the oil, such as cities in the United States, Europe, India, and China. Huge oceangoing ships called tankers carry oil throughout the world's shipping lanes. Some tankers can hold as much as 42 million gallons (159 million liters) of **crude oil.**

Oil spills

Although most operators of tankers are well trained and safety conscious, tanker accidents occasionally do happen at sea. If the tanker is breached (broken open), millions of gallons of oil can spill into the water and wash up on nearby shores. The effect of an oil spill can be catastrophic. Oil poisons marine animals such as fish, shellfish, otters, and seals. It soaks shorelines, killing tiny sand-living animals. The feathers of sea birds become soaked and clogged with oil, and the birds suffocate, drown, or die of toxic exposure. Some of the oil soaks into seabeds or shorelines, which can remain toxic for many years.

Thermal pollution

Thermal is from the same root word as *thermometer* and refers to heating or warming. **Thermal pollution** is caused by heated water discharged into rivers, lakes, or streams. Even though the water may be clean, its high temperature can disrupt the lives of living things.

Power plants use water from nearby sources to keep parts of their equipment from overheating. Cool water is passed through pipes, and heat is transferred from working parts of machines to the water. Then the hot water is discharged from the plant.

Heated water can affect living things in several ways. Because warm water cannot hold as much dissolved oxygen as cool water, it can harm fish and marine plants by reducing the amount of dissolved oxygen in the water. It may also confuse fish that rely on seasonal temperature changes to locate their breeding grounds. If the water is hot enough, it can cause fish and other organisms to go into shock and die.

This map shows the location of the 20 largest oil spills in history. It also shows the location of the *Exxon Valdez* spill, the largest oil spill in U.S. history.

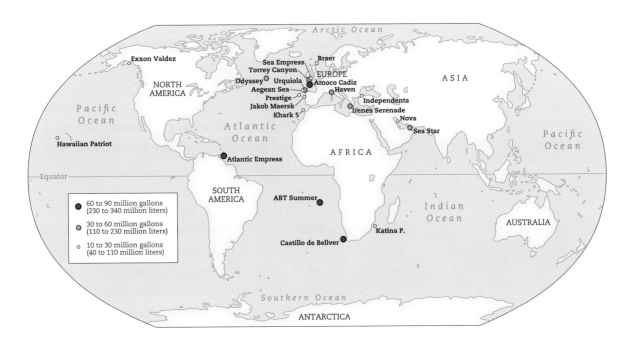

Workers try to clean green algae from a lake in China. Agricultural pollution can cause huge algal blooms that kill fish and other wildlife.

WATER POLLUTION FROM AGRICULTURE

Agriculture includes all the ways in which farmers raise crops and animals. Like other human activities, agriculture today has become highly industrialized—that is, practiced on a large scale with modern technology. Farmers farm huge tracts of land and use chemical **fertilizers** to create highly productive harvests. They use chemical **pesticides** to control insects, **fungicides** to control diseases, and **herbicides** to kill weeds.

In time, many agricultural chemicals are washed by rainwater into streams and rivers. River systems carry the chemicals into bays, gulfs, or oceans. Because of this agricultural runoff, high concentrations of chemicals tend to collect in coastal waters, which provide much of the seafood that people eat. Clams, oysters, shrimp, crabs, and a variety of fish live and grow in these waters.

Chemicals such as pesticides and herbicides may directly poison marine animals. However, dissolved fertilizers can cause severe harm in a different way. These fertilizers introduce nutrients that encourage rapid growth of some kinds of algae, small plantlike water organisms. When prompted by such nutrients, algae can multiply into huge populations. Such an event is called an **algal bloom**. The algae form dense masses on water surfaces, blocking out sunlight. As more algae grow, more algae die, and the bacteria that **decompose** (break down) the dead algae use up the oxygen in the water, which other water animals rely upon. Some types of algae also give off toxins. Algal blooms can kill off huge numbers of fish, shellfish, and other organisms.

Other contributors to pollution by nutrient runoff are "factory farms" that raise huge numbers of poultry, pigs, cattle, and other animals on small areas of land. Disposal of the animal wastes poses a serious environmental problem. In many cases, the farm operations collect and store animal wastes in ponds called lagoons. Wastes in a lagoon may wash or leak out due to weak dams or heavy rainfall. Like chemical fertilizer, animal waste promotes growth of harmful algae in coastal waters.

Factory farms house thousands of hogs. Their waste is held in giant lagoons, which can leak into water supplies.

What Is Water Pollution?   45

Water pollution from untreated sewage can cause outbreaks of disease. Dozens of people in Zimbabwe died in 2006 from an outbreak of cholera caused by sewage.

WATER POLLUTION FROM SEWAGE

Sewage is water that contains waste matter produced by human beings. It comes from the sinks and toilets of homes, restaurants, office buildings, and factories. Sewage typically contains small amounts of solid material and dissolved material that cannot be seen. Most sewage also includes disease-producing bacteria and harmful chemicals. The chemicals may come from factories or other industries, or they may come from cleaning chemicals in homes.

Many towns and cities have waste treatment plants that use scientific methods to remove toxins and kill germs in wastewater. In many parts of the world, however, raw (untreated) sewage is dumped into bodies of water, where it kills fish and plants.

Both raw and treated sewage can increase nutrients in bodies of water to unsafe levels. Just like agricultural wastes, sewage can promote the growth of harmful algae that deplete the dissolved oxygen in water and kill off other organisms.

The spread of disease

One of the largest unmet needs in today's world is enough safe, clean drinking water. Many developing countries do not have modern water systems and sewage treatment plants. People in villages and towns in many areas of the world must draw their water from rivers, streams, or unreliable wells.

One of the main dangers of drinking untreated, unclean water is getting sick from waterborne diseases such as cholera (*KOL uhr uh*), a bacterial disease of the intestines. The chief symptom is diarrhea, and without proper medical care, people can die of dehydration (the lack of sufficient water for the body to function) caused by diarrhea.

According to the World Health Organization (WHO), nearly 2 million people worldwide die each year from cholera and related waterborne diseases. WHO experts estimate that nearly 90 percent of these diseases are caused by unsafe water supplies and could be prevented.

Typhoid fever is another waterborne bacterial disease that often afflicts people who do not have access to clean drinking water. Typhoid fever can cause high fevers and death. Schistosomiasis (SHIHS *tuh soh MY uh sihs*) is a serious, sometimes fatal disease caused by tiny worms carried in unclean water. It occurs chiefly in sub-Saharan Africa.

Cholera, typhoid, and schistosomiasis are entirely preventable diseases. However, they cannot always be prevented in rural areas and communities that do not have safe drinking water. Each of these diseases is often spread by sewage that contaminates drinking water. Such contamination occurs most often in low-lying places where ground water is very near the surface. Without safe water and sewer systems, sewage can seep through the ground and into water wells.

GREEN FACT

The World Health Organization estimates that approximately 290,589 gallons (1.1 million liters) of raw sewage are dumped into the Ganges River in India every minute.

Scientists and public health officials test water supplies to see if they contain dangerous microorganisms.

Many pollutants end up in the oceans. The tuna in this fishing boat's nets are likely contaminated with mercury, a toxic heavy metal.

THE HEALTH OF THE OCEANS

Oceans cover nearly 71 percent of Earth's surface and contain 97 percent of all the water on Earth. Because the oceans are so vast, people once believed that these bodies of water could continually absorb pollution without serious damage. However, scientists are now finding that the oceans are more fragile than once thought.

Ocean waters are salty and cannot be used for drinking water without a costly process called **desalination**, which removes the salt. However, the oceans contain a tremendous variety of life, from one-celled organisms to huge squids and whales. Populations of many ocean species are declining, either through the effects of overfishing or from pollution.

Nutrient-laden waters

Nutrients in fertilizers from farms and in sewage from towns and cities wash into rivers and eventually into bays and oceans. These materials prompt the sudden appearance of algal blooms. The masses of algae cause oxygen to become depleted from the water underneath. As a result, marine animals in the area either flee or suffocate, creating a **dead zone**. In the early 2000's, scientists identified more than 50 dead zones in coastal waters around the world. Some of the dead zones are seasonal in nature. Every spring and summer, a large dead zone develops in the Gulf of Mexico as the Mississippi River carries increasing amounts of agricultural runoff into the sea. In autumn, the dead zone fades away as currents in the Gulf spread and thin out the nutrient wastes.

Heavy metals

Heavy metals, such as arsenic, lead, and mercury, are especially harmful to living things. These toxins are released from power plants, chemical plants, mining operations, and other sources.

Plastic litter is harmful to the oceans because it does not break down easily. Sea birds, turtles, seals, whales, and other sea creatures can get tangled in plastic nets, bags, and packing material. Marine animals sometimes eat plastic, mistaking it for food. Plastic can block up an animal's digestive system, causing it to starve to death. Plastic litter also washes up on shorelines, making beach environments less attractive.

They dissolve in water and are carried hundreds or thousands of miles in rivers and streams into the oceans. Heavy metals tend to accumulate in the ocean food chain such that large, predatory fish can carry dangerous amounts of these toxins. The tragedy in Minamata, Japan, in the mid-1900's was a stark demonstration of how dangerous heavy metal pollution in the oceans can be (see page 37).

Garbage dumped into the ocean can wash ashore, polluting beaches and threatening wildlife.

Acidification

Emissions from power plants, factories, and automobiles can re-combine with moisture in the **atmosphere** to form **acid rain.** Acid rain causes widespread damage on land, but it is also a threat to the oceans. The same clouds that pour acid rain over land also move over oceans. Also, acid rain on land eventually washes into rivers and streams and, in time, flows into oceans.

Acid can also form in ocean water by chemical reactions with **carbon dioxide** in the air. The amount of carbon dioxide in Earth's atmosphere has risen over time. As carbon dioxide levels rise, the ocean's acidity level rises as well.

Many scientists believe that Earth's oceans have already become slightly more acidic over the last century. If the oceans continue to acidify, some marine plants and animals will begin to die off. The more acidic the water becomes, the fewer organisms will be able to survive.

What Is Water Pollution? 49

When levees failed following Hurricane Katrina, most of New Orleans flooded. Those floodwaters covered the city in toxic chemicals.

WHEN NATURAL DISASTER STRIKES

The harmful effects of existing pollution can be greatly magnified by natural disasters. The people of the United States became aware of this grim reality in the wake of Hurricane Katrina, which devastated the city of New Orleans and other parts of the Louisiana and Mississippi Gulf coasts in August 2005.

Katrina moved into the New Orleans area from the Gulf of Mexico in the early morning hours of August 29, 2005. After the hurricane's center passed New Orleans, its accompanying storm surge battered the city's levees (walls that hold back water) and broke or overtopped them at several points. Because much of New Orleans is below sea level, the overflowing water quickly flooded about 80 percent of the city's land area.

New Orleans remained flooded—and mostly abandoned—for weeks. The floodwaters remained standing for so long that they absorbed and spread toxic substances from the area. The full extent of the contamination may never be fully known.

In Katrina's wake, environmental experts were especially concerned that at least five Superfund sites in southeastern Louisiana and coastal Mississippi had been flooded. (For more information about the Superfund program, see page 53.) In New Orleans itself, several sources of polluting toxins were identified, but little could be done to limit the damage until the floodwaters were pumped out. Two miles north of the city's central business district, the Agriculture Street **landfill** leached toxins as standing water broke through a layer of protective sheeting.

Flooding caused by Hurricane Katrina spread a toxic brew of pollutants over much of New Orleans, complicating recovery efforts.

At the Meraux **refinery** in St. Bernard Parish, owned by Murphy Oil USA, Inc., a huge above-ground oil storage tank was dislodged and split open by the force of moving water, spilling more than 1 million gallons (3.8 million liters) of crude oil into the swirling floodwaters. Experts estimated that 1,200 neighboring houses were badly polluted by the oil slick.

Also of great concern to environmental experts was the U.S. Naval Construction Battalion Center in Gulfport, Mississippi, which had been flooded by Katrina. In the late 1960's and 1970's, the facility was used to store the herbicide Agent Orange, which was used to strip jungles of leaves during the Vietnam War. Over time, the herbicide had leaked from some ruptured drums into nearby soil, releasing dioxin. Soil samples from the area taken after Katrina showed dioxin levels that were above the recommended levels.

A CLOSER LOOK
Where Did Our Wetlands Go?

A wetland, such as a swamp, marsh, or bog, is an area where the soil remains waterlogged for much of the year. Wetlands are like sponges, absorbing large amounts of water. When wetlands are abundant and healthy, the tremendous amount of water released by a hurricane—whether from a storm surge or rainfall—can be partly absorbed by wetlands. After Hurricane Katrina struck in 2005, scientists noted that southeastern Louisiana had lost vast tracts of wetlands to development since 1960. They speculated that New Orleans might have escaped harm if the wetlands had been present to soak up Katrina's surge.

Cleanup and Prevention

Section Summary

Cleanup and Prevention

Scientists continue to develop chemicals, tools, and machines to help clean up pollution. However, reducing pollution is even more important. Governments can help by posing limits on the amount of emissions industries can produce. Industries can help by switching to cleaner forms of energy. Individuals can help by reducing their own energy use.

Oil spills in the ocean are especially devastating for birds that live on the shore, such as these penguins in South Africa.

Factories flush chemicals into waterways. Agricultural runoff gathers in bays and triggers toxic **algal blooms**. An oil tanker breaks up in a fierce storm and huge quantities of oil wash up on nearby beaches.

Preventing any of these environmental catastrophes is highly desirable. However, people must be prepared to respond to accidents that do happen.

Cleanup methods

Scientists and engineers continue to develop **remediation methods** to deal with catastrophic pollution. Remediation means "cleaning up," and pollution remediation methods draw on state-of-the-art technology to clean up land, sea, and air harmed by pollution. Today, one of the fastest-growing engineering fields is environmental engineering, which specializes in pollution remediation.

A large oil spill can catastrophically pollute coastal ocean beds and shorelines. Scientists work hard to develop technology to clean up oil spills as efficiently and thoroughly as possible. Volunteers pitch in by rescuing and cleaning sea birds and other animals. The "Closer Look" box on page 53 describes some remediation methods currently used on oil spills.

Government action

Governments have the power to **regulate** the activities of private corporations. In democratic countries, citizens decide what the governmental policies will be. An important way to control polluting activities is for the government to mandate (demand) reductions in pollution produced by industries.

In 1970, the United States Congress passed the Clean Air Act. It set guidelines for developing cleaner-burning fuels and required the U.S. automobile industry to develop vehicles with better gas mileage. In 1972, Congress passed the Clean Water Act, which established laws to reduce or eliminate water pollution. Many of these laws were directed at big industrial polluters such as chemical plants and **smelters.** Since the early 1970's, Congress has amended (changed) the Clean Air and Clean Water acts to bring environmental laws in line with new or changing pollution issues.

State governments take action, too. In July 2007, North Carolina passed a law that banned the construction or expansion of lagoons on hog farms. North Carolina's waterways were severely polluted after Hurricane Floyd struck eastern North Carolina in 1999. The flooding caused some hog lagoons to rupture, releasing the wastewater into the coastal sounds and ocean inlets and creating a 40-square-mile (104-square-kilometer) **dead zone** in Pamlico Sound.

The Superfund

In December 1980, Congress passed the Comprehensive Environmental Response, Compensation, and Liability Act, which President Jimmy Carter signed into law. The law is popularly known as the "Superfund." Prompted in part by the Love Canal disaster, the Superfund provided billions of dollars to clean up toxic waste sites in the United States and authorized the **Environmental Protection Agency (EPA)** to oversee the program.

Since 1980, the Superfund legislation has accomplished the cleanup of nearly 1,000 toxic sites. However, about 500 new toxic sites come to the attention of the EPA each year. In 1995, Congress let the funding for the Superfund program expire. Originally, the program was set up to charge the polluters for most of the cleanup costs. Without Congressional approval for the funding, however, most of the cleanup efforts are now paid for by taxpayers rather than polluters.

Environmental workers testing soil

WHAT YOU CAN DO

Most scientists believe that Earth has suffered substantial damage from human-made pollution. However, it is never too late to change practices and patterns of behavior that pollute. Preventing pollution is much more efficient and effective than cleaning it up. People around the world can take serious steps to cut down their use of goods and services that add to **carbon dioxide** already in the **atmosphere.** Some of these steps are considered in the "Closer Look" box on page 55.

Reducing your carbon footprint

It's easy to form a mental image of your footprint, but what is a **carbon footprint**? Each of us is a consumer of energy and goods. Every time we use electric power or some other form of energy, or use a product that is made in a factory, we contribute in a small way to carbon dioxide build-up in the atmosphere. The *carbon* in *carbon footprint* stands for carbon dioxide, which is measured in tons (gases, like solids, have weight). So your carbon footprint is the weight of all of the carbon dioxide your actions cause to be released into the atmosphere over one year.

People in the United States are big consumers of energy. The average carbon footprint of a U.S. citizen is nearly 24 metric tons of carbon dioxide per year. In the United Kingdom, the average carbon footprint is 12 metric tons.

There are many ways in which citizens can reduce their carbon footprint. These changes, though fairly small, could make a great difference if multiplied across Earth's billions of people.

Recycling

Recycling is a "green" way to handle the waste that would otherwise clog **landfills.** People use huge amounts of products made from such recyclable materials as metal, glass, paper, and plastic. Plastic, which is made partly from oil, does not break down quickly, making it especially important to recycle this material. As plastic trash piles up, it becomes a large pollution problem.

Making products from recycled materials often takes less energy than making them from new materials. It also reduces the amount of natural resources we use. Old paper items can be

People can help reduce pollution by using energy-efficient light bulbs, taking public transportation, and recycling.

recycled and made into new paper products, such as writing paper. Recycled aluminum cans are melted and made into new aluminum cans.

"Green" business practices

Industries and other businesses also share in the responsibility for preventing pollution. Some businesses that have traditionally been big polluters are beginning to turn to more environmentally friendly practices. Industries that give off high **emissions**—such as smelters and coal-burning power plants—incorporate high-tech **scrubbers** into their smokestacks to remove harmful sulfur and nitrates. Smelters and chemical plants use technology to recycle wastes back into their processes again and again, reducing the output of pollution.

Some government agencies and corporations mandate that their vehicles be fueled with E-85. E-85 is a fuel blend of 85 percent **ethanol** and 15 percent gasoline. E-85 burns more cleanly than pure gasoline. These governments and companies set trends for reduced fuel consumption in the hope that the general public will follow. If everyone reduced their use of gasoline, it would cut down on the production of greenhouse gases and other **pollutants**.

Recycling plastic saves energy and reduces the amount of waste going into landfills.

A CLOSER LOOK
Reducing Your Carbon Footprint

Here are ways you can reduce your family's carbon footprint at home.

- Turn off lights not being used.

- Switch to energy-efficient light bulbs.

- If your home has an old furnace, encourage your family to replace it with a more energy-efficient one.

- Keep the thermostat at 78 °F (25.6 °C) in summer and 68 °F (20 °C) in winter.

- Encourage your family to replace its standard car with a hybrid-electric car.

- Take public transportation whenever possible.

- Walk or ride a bicycle whenever possible.

- Encourage your family to travel by train or bus on long trips, rather than by jet.

- Recycle cans from beverages. Cans are made from aluminum, and producing aluminum takes a great deal of energy.

- Use a laptop instead of a desktop computer, or use your library's or school's computers.

Higher temperatures in the Arctic could doom polar bears if the ocean's surface ice disappears.

THE CHALLENGE OF GLOBAL WARMING

The amount of carbon dioxide in Earth's atmosphere is increasing today and has been increasing for about the past 200 years. Many scientists believe that this human-caused increase in carbon dioxide and other greenhouse gases is causing **global warming.**

In 2007, a scientific study panel sponsored by the **United Nations (UN)** issued a report on global warming. In the report, the scientists estimated that Earth's surface temperature had warmed by 1.33 °F (0.74 °C) between 1906 and 2005. Many scientists believe that the rate of warming is speeding up today. Some estimate that over the coming century, Earth could warm up by as much as 11.5 °F (6.4 °C). Such a rise in Earth's temperature would bring about catastrophic change, including a rise in sea levels and flooding of many coastal regions.

Kyoto Protocol

Many people, both political leaders and individuals, are beginning to take action to slow down global warming. In 1997, world leaders gathered in Kyoto, Japan, and passed an international protocol (statement of agreement) on actions to take to reduce global warming. The protocol, called the **Kyoto Protocol**, set limits for the amount of carbon dioxide and other greenhouse gases that countries could produce. It also suggested that the world community set up ways to trade **carbon credits**. A carbon credit is permission to produce a certain amount of greenhouse gas. Countries that produce less carbon dioxide than their Kyoto limits could then trade (sell) some of their leftover carbon credits to other countries. This system of exchange of carbon credits is known as **cap and trade**, and it provides an economic motivation for countries to avoid producing carbon dioxide.

Most of the world's countries ratified (agreed to) the Kyoto Protocol. However, Australia did not ratify the protocol until 2007, and the United States has not ratified it.

Cap-and-trade systems

Nations and communities are taking the basic ideas of the Kyoto Protocol a step further. They are setting up cap-and-trade systems at the national or community level. In these systems, businesses and even individuals receive carbon credits. They then make choices about how much fuel, electric power, heating oil, or other carbon-dioxide-producing products they will use. People or businesses who **conserve** energy and have credits left over can sell them to bigger energy consumers.

The government of the Republic of Ireland is developing a cap-and-trade plan for fuel use there. Under the plan, the number of carbon credits issued would match commitments Irish leaders have made in international agreements such as the Kyoto Protocol. The government would set up a market where the carbon credits could be traded.

Many environmentalists and economists think that, in time, national or global "carbon markets"—rather like today's stock markets—will be set up to trade carbon credits. The carbon markets would thereby help control emissions of carbon dioxide and other greenhouse gases. Such a system could help the world's people significantly reduce the harmful build-up of carbon dioxide in the atmosphere.

Many people want governments to do more to slow down global warming. Below, protesters gather outside the 2005 UN Climate Change Conference in Montreal, Canada.

Activities

EXPERIMENT: CLEANING UP OIL SPILLS

Introduction

As you can learn in this book, oil is a toxic material that can harm plant and animal life. Oil spills are very difficult to clean up, so scientists have developed special tools, machines, and detergents to break up the oil to help repair the environment. Try this experiment to see how detergents help with oil spills.

Materials:

- Small amount of oil (such as vegetable, olive, or any household oil)
- Household detergent
- Glass jar with lid, filled halfway with water

Directions:

1. Add several drops of oil to the jar of water.
2. Screw on the lid and shake the jar for several seconds. Did the oil mix with the water?
3. Add several drops of detergent to the jar. Screw on the lid and shake the jar for several seconds. What happened to the oil?

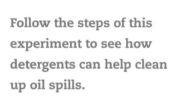

Follow the steps of this experiment to see how detergents can help clean up oil spills.

RESEARCH PROJECT: FIND THE AIR QUALITY INDEX FOR YOUR COUNTRY

Introduction:

Many governments use an Air Quality Index (AQI) to provide information about air quality in different regions of the country. The AQI in the United States measures five types of pollution: **ozone** pollution, particle pollution (also called **particulate** matter), **carbon monoxide**, sulfur dioxide, and nitrogen dioxide.

The AQI can be shown as a chart or map and uses colors, numbers, and words to show the air quality for an area. The chart on page 59 shows the categories used for the AQI in the United States.

Directions:

1. Ask your teacher or public or school librarian to help you look up the air quality index for your country on the Internet. The URL links to AQI's for several countries are listed below.

2. Look at the map or chart to find the areas that are the most polluted. Why do you think some areas are more polluted than others?

Air Quality Index (AQI) Values	Levels of Health Concern	Colors
When the AQI is in this range:	...air quality conditions are:	...as symbolized by this color:
0 to 50	Good	Green
51 to 100	Moderate	Yellow
101 to 150	Unhealthy for sensitive groups	Orange
151 to 200	Unhealthy	Red
201 to 300	Very unhealthy	Purple
301 to 500	Hazardous	Maroon

Source: AIRNow.gov.

Air Quality Indexes

United States:

http://cfpub.epa.gov/airnow/index.cfm?action=airnow.national

Canada:

http://airnow.gov/index.cfm?action=airnow.canadamaps

United Kingdom:

http://www.airquality.co.uk/archive/index.php

Australia:

(New South Wales)

http://www.environment.nsw.gov.au/airqual/web24hsum.asp

(EPA Victoria)

http://www.epa.vic.gov.au/air/aq4kids/station_map.asp

You can find a list of links to more air quality indexes at http://airnow.gov/index.cfm?action=airnow.world.

Glossary

acid rain rain that has a high concentration of acids because of air pollution.

aerated liquid a liquid that has formed a fine spray light enough to stay in the air.

algal bloom a sudden, abnormal explosion of the population of algae in a body of water caused by large amounts of nutrients in the water.

atmosphere the mixture of gases in contact with Earth's surface and extending far above.

biofuel a liquid fuel made from plant matter, animal waste, or other biological sources.

biosphere the collection of all places on Earth in which life can dwell.

by-product an additional product created in the manufacture of an object or substance.

cap and trade a system that creates a market in pollution credits.

carbon credit permission to produce a certain amount of greenhouse gas.

carbon dioxide a colorless, odorless gas given off by burning and by animals breathing out.

carbon footprint the total amount of carbon dioxide given off by a particular human acitivity.

carbon monoxide a toxic, colorless and odorless gas.

conserve to keep from harm or loss; preserve.

crude oil the form of oil that comes directly out of the ground; petroleum.

dead zone an area in the ocean with too little oxygen for plant and animal life to survive.

decompose to break down; decay.

desalination the process of removing salt from salt water such as ocean water.

electron an extremely tiny particle in atoms that carries a negative charge.

emission an airborne waste product.

Environmental Protection Agency (EPA) the federal agency that works to protect the U.S. environment from pollution.

erosion gradual wearing away by wind, rain, ice, or other forces.

ethanol a widely used biofuel made from plants or algae; ethyl alcohol.

exhaust partially burned gases, such as those given off by most automobiles when they are running.

fertilizer a substance that helps plants to grow.

food chain a group of interrelated organisms in which each member of the group feeds upon the one below it and is in turn eaten by the organism above it.

fossil fuel underground deposits that were formed millions of years ago from the remains of plants and animals. Coal, oil, and natural gas are fossil fuels.

freight goods carried by a form of transportation.

fungicide a poison that kills fungal pests.

global warming the gradual warming of Earth's surface, believed to be caused by a build-up of greenhouse gases in the atmosphere.

greenhouse gas any gas that contributes to the greenhouse effect.

greenhouse effect the process by which certain gases cause the Earth's atmosphere to warm.

ground water water that pools underground in porous rocks.

habitat the place where an animal or plant naturally lives or grows.

hazardous waste a material that can endanger human health or damage the environment.

heavy metal a metal such as lead, mercury, and arsenic, which can collect in the tissues of organisms and is toxic to most living things.

herbicide a poison that kills weeds.

hydrocarbon a chemical compound containing carbon and hydrogen.

hydroelectric power plant a power plant that develops electric power from water power.

incineration the act of burning thoroughly.

industrial production the process of making goods on a very large scale.

Kyoto Protocol the international agreement that set limits for the amount of greenhouse gases that countries can produce.

landfill a place where trash and other solid waste materials are discarded.

nitrogen oxide a compound of nitrogen and oxygen.

nuclear power plant a power plant that develops electric power from radioactive material.

organic chemical a chemical compound that contains carbon atoms.

ozone a form of oxygen gas.

particulate a tiny piece of solid material that floats in the air.

persistent organic pollutants (POP's) a group of dangerous synthetic organic chemicals.

pesticide a poison that kills pests such as insects.

petroleum another name for the fossil fuel often called oil.

pollutant a single source of pollution.

power grid the interconnected system of power plants, transmission wires, and end-users of electric power.

refinery a factory in which useful products such as gasoline are extracted from crude oil.

regulate to control by rule, principle, or system.

remediation method a technology-assisted method of cleaning up pollution on land, in the sea, or in the air.

reproductive having to do with the ways in which organisms copy and perpetuate themselves.

river system a river and all the tributaries (smaller streams) that flow into it.

scrubber an air pollution control system that filters out harmful pollutants from emissions in power plants and factories.

sewage water that contains waste matter produced by human beings.

sick building syndrome (SBS) conditions of air quality that develop when air inside a building is continually stale and polluted.

smelter a type of chemical factory in which metals are extracted from rocky material called ore.

smog a brown, hazy mixture of gases and particulates caused by exhaust gases released by automobiles and other users of fossil fuels.

synthetic human-made.

tailings pond a pond containing toxic liquid wastes from smelting operations.

thermal pollution the effect of heated water (which may be clean) that has been discharged into rivers, lakes, or streams.

turbine a wheellike object that spins around and around.

ultraviolet rays the invisible rays in the part of the spectrum beyond the violet.

United Nations an international organization that works for world peace and human prosperity.

ventilation regular exchange of stale air for fresh air.

Additional Resources

WEB SITES

AIRNow
http://www.airnow.gov

A government-backed program that offers much information about pollution; includes a student page, "Kid's Air."

Air Pollution: What's the Solution?
http://www.ciese.org/curriculum/airproj

An educational project for grades K-12 that uses online, real-time data to guide student discovery of the science behind the causes and effects of outdoor air pollution.

Blacksmith Institute
http://www.blacksmithinstitute.org

Works to solve pollution problems in the developing world; includes list of the world's most polluted places with links.

Canadian Environmental Assessment Agency
http://www.ceaa-acee.gc.ca

Provides environmental assessments that contribute to well-informed decision making; supports sustainable development.

Environment Agency
http://www.environment-agency.gov.uk

Provides tools to make the environment a better place for you and for future generations; includes resources for schools.

Science Daily Pollution News
http://www.sciencedaily.com/news/earth_climate/pollution

Contains the latest and most pertinent pollution information; updated daily.

Scorecard
http://www.scorecard.org

Provides answers to the most common inquiries on pollution; includes comparisons of pollution among U.S. states and communities.

United States Environmental Protection Agency
http://www.epa.gov

Contains much information on pollution and the environment; includes a student page.

Water Pollution Guide
http://www.water-pollution.org.uk

Offers information about the sources of water pollution and how they can be treated.

World News: Pollution
http://www.wn.com/pollution

Contains lots of pollution information in an easily navigable format.

BOOKS

Air Pollution
by J. S. and Renee A. Kidd (Chelsea House, 2006)

Earth's Garbage Crisis
by Christiane Dorion (World Almanac Library, 2007)

Pollution
by Louise I. Gerdes, ed., (Greenhaven 2006)

Pollution A to Z
by Richard M. Stapleton, ed. (Macmillan Reference, 2004)

This Is My Planet
by Jan Thornhill (Maple Tree Press, 2007)

Index